The Order of Life

foreword by

PASTOR BEN DOWDING

The
Order
of Life

*The Pathway to Living
a Fulfilled Life*

DOUGLAS ASANTE

To the One who is the true foundation of all order
— God Almighty, my Father, Friend,
and First Priority.

To my beloved wife, Diana, your unwavering love,
patience, and partnership have been a living
testament to the beauty of godly order in the home.

To my amazing daughters, Dasha, Daphne
and Danelle, you are my joy and daily inspiration.
May your lives always reflect the grace, strength,
and wisdom of walking in divine alignment.

And to every reader hungry for a life of meaning
—May this book lead you into the fullness
of God's purpose, where peace and fulfilment
are not dreams, but daily realities.

Contents

Acknowledgements

First and foremost, I return all glory to God Almighty, the Author of life and the Giver of wisdom. He inspired the vision, gave me the burden, and carried me through every stage of writing this book. *The Order of Life* is His message—I am only a vessel.

To my loving wife, Dr. (Mrs) Diana Ama Asante, thank you for your unwavering support, your steadfast prayers, and your deep belief in the calling upon my life. Your love has been my constant strength and comfort.

To my amazing children, Dasha, Daphne and Danelle, you are a blessing from the Lord and daily reminders of God's grace and purpose in my life. I pray this book becomes a legacy for you and your generation.

To Ps Ben Dowding, thank you for honouring me by writing the foreword to this book. Your words brought clarity, strength, and depth to this message, and I am deeply grateful.

To my fellow pastors in the work of the ministry—Rev. Mike Tembo and Ps Nana Asante—thank you for your friendship, leadership, encouragement, and example. It is a great joy and honour to serve alongside you. Your lives reflect the very truths this book proclaims.

To Christian Family Ministry, thank you for standing with me, praying for me, and cheering me on. Your words of affirmation, intercession, and presence in my life are invaluable.

To those who graciously endorsed this book—..... (please add) thank you for honouring me with your kind words and standing behind this work. Your voices amplify the message and mission of this book.

To the incredible team at Equip Publishing House, thank you for your commitment to excellence and kingdom impact. You helped bring this vision into reality with clarity, professionalism, and heart.

Finally, to every reader, seeker, leader, and lover of truth— thank you for picking up this book. May the truths contained in these pages reorder your life, rekindle your purpose, and reignite your walk with God.

This is more than a book—it is a call back to divine alignment. To God alone be all the glory.

Endorsements

A profound spiritual compass for navigating life's complexities. Every believer should engage with this book to realign their priorities with God's divine order.

REV. CHRISTA AFFUL
International Centre for Prayer Ministries

This is another master piece from Pastor Douglas bringing insights from a father and a Pastors perspective to strengthen our deep dependency on God. I recommend this book as a tool for all and local churches as a resource for teaching new parents.

REV. JK FORSON CF
British Army Chaplain

Apostle Douglas Asante's book, *"The Order of Life: The Pathway to Living a Fulfilled Life,"* challenges the common reliance on survival instincts, passion, and self-actualisation as life drivers—career, family, or ministry—arguing that deviating from God's design leads to wasted years without fulfillment. Instead, he presents three biblically rooted priorities in a specific order: Seeking God, Family Life, and Purpose, using Job's life as a key example. The book offers practical, doctrinally sound, and Spirit-filled wisdom for achieving true fulfillment on earth, making it a timeless must-read that will remain relevant for generations if Christ delays His return.

REV. DR. RICHARD GYASI KWAA
Kings Destiny Church International
Pastor and Author

The Order of Life is a timely and transformative guide that illuminates the pathway to living a truly fulfilled life. Rich with practical wisdom rooted in faith, it calls us to prioritise our relationship with God, nurture a healthy family life, and pursue our purpose with diligence and balance. More than just a book, it is a compelling roadmap for anyone determined to live meaningfully, navigate competing demands, and leave a lasting legacy.

REV. NANA KOFI ASIEDU APPIAH
Pharmacist

Foreword

From the very outset of this book, Pastor Douglas poses a question that is as profound as it is personal—a question that every one of us, regardless of background or station in life, must one day face. From the highest academic intellect to those who feel themselves far removed from scholarly pursuits, countless men and women across the centuries have wrestled with this very enquiry, often embarking on long and arduous journeys in pursuit of its answer.

The question is this:

What does personal fulfilment mean to you?

More than twenty-five years ago, my wife and I (then newly engaged) embarked on a journey of full-time ministry. At that time, we had little idea of the incredible adventure that lay ahead of us. Yet even at the very beginning, a scripture came alive in our hearts, shaping the course of our lives and becoming the unshakable centre of our faith, family, finances, friendships, focus, and fulfilment:

> *"But seek first his kingdom and his righteousness,*
> *and all these things will be given to you as well."*
> MATTHEW 6:33 (NIV)

Over this past quarter of a century, we have experienced the remarkable favour of God, time and again, as we have chosen to step out in faith and walk in obedience to His call. What began as a simple pursuit of putting God first has grown into the privilege of witnessing churches planted and established across the nation of England.

Through this journey, one of the greatest truths we have discovered—sometimes forgotten and then graciously rediscovered—is that genuine fulfilment does not come from chasing the shifting priorities and promises of the world. Instead, it flows from faithfulness and obedience to the call of God and to the gentle leading of His Spirit. It is as we allow His guidance to permeate every aspect of life that we begin to walk the pathway of true fulfilment.

Discovering fulfilment begins with discovering our divine design. It is about recognising how the Creator has uniquely fashioned us and how He longs for us to know Him more deeply. In doing so, we unlock a clearer sense of purpose and direction that transforms not only our spiritual walk but also the practical outworking of our daily lives.

In *The Order of Life*, Pastor Douglas draws from biblical insight and personal revelation to illuminate these very truths. His teaching will both challenge and inspire, helping you to grow in your understanding of God's design for fulfilment and how it is outworked in a life of devotion.

Everyone desires fruitfulness, yet few are willing to embrace the cost of faithfulness. Pastor Douglas has embodied this principle in both his life and ministry. Through this book, he offers invaluable keys that will enable others to discover the same enduring truth for themselves.

+ If you are seeking clarity of purpose...
+ If you long to make a meaningful difference with your life...
+ If you desire to live in the abundance of fulfilment that God promises...

Then this book is for you. *The Order of Life* will not only guide you into biblical principles of fulfilment but will also show you how to live them out in service to God and His Kingdom.

PASTOR BEN DOWDING
Senior Minister, Influence Church

Introduction

How would you define fulfilment? What does personal fulfilment mean to you? What indicators would you use to jugde that one is fulfilled, taking into consideration the person's life, ministry, or business? Of what need is fulfilment in life? Does being happy with yourself translate to fulfilment? All these questions and more about fulfilment come to mind when you doubt what to do with your life or when you seek to do something more meaningful in life.

The quest for fulfilment is ultimate in every ones' life. It determines our happiness, purpose and sense of direction in life. If living a fulfilled were not important, then there would be no reason to live at all. You need a sense of fulfilment to enjoy life in this busy world where many feel unhappy with their lives, though successful.

Success in life does not equate fulfilment. You might be a successful athlete; yet, you may not have a sense of fulfilment. Have you never come across artistes, businessmen, among others, who, though successful, are not happy with their lives? They have a vacuum in them; they know something is missing in their life, and that thing is what they really quest for.

Often, people take success and fulfilment to mean the same thing. While anybody can be successful if they learn to work hard, fulfilment, on the other hand, is not a function of hard work. Fulfilment is a sense of inner peace, happiness and contentment with what you love to do, whether it brings you reward or not. In other words, success is tied to the money, the car, the house and every material thing you gain from working, while fulfilment is tied to your purpose in life.

God's primary intention at creation was that humanity would have dominion over all that He had created (Gen 1:26). This dominion is not limited to a place, thing, or possession. This dominion mandate is a complete package that God put in you. Until you discover your purpose, it would be difficult to find fulfilment. In God's agenda, your fulfilment is not restricted to just an aspect of your life. Fulfilment is you finding purpose in life through God. You are not to go seeking after success. It should be part of your life when you find purpose. Therefore, seek fulfilment rather than working tirelessly to become successful.

The Bible says:

> 'Then God blessed them, and God said to them, "Be fruitful and multiply; fill the earth and subdue it; have dominion over the fish of the sea, over the birds of the air, and over every living thing that moves on the earth."'
> GENESIS 1:28

There are some keywords we need to look at in the above Bible text. They were God's original command to humanity. God defines fulfilment based on those words.

First, He said *be fruitful*. You become fruitful when your life flourishes and becomes a blessing to others. A fruitful tree is not only a blessed tree, but it becomes a source of blessing to humanity and shelter to other living creatures. A tree can never be fruitful until it remains connected to the soil where it gets its nourishment. Likewise, a life will never be fruitful until it remains with the source—God. Fruitfulness and fulfilment will become your reality so long as you stay with God. In searching for God, you will find yourself.

God's plan for you is not just for you to live in comfort and affluence only, but that your life becomes an extension of heaven on earth. The Bible says, for the kingdom of God is not eating and drinking, but righteousness and peace and joy in the Holy Spirit (Romans 14:17).

Merriment and pleasure do not bring fulfilment. It takes seeking the kingdom of God, which produces righteousness, peace and joy, to have a true sense of life, and this is what a fruitful life must reflect. Fulfilment is not complete until you become an answer to human's question or a solution to humanity's problem.

The second of God's commandment of fulfilment is to *multiply*. Multiplication is a vast increment without bounds or limits. God sees fulfilment as multiplication, whereby the little *you* becomes great, and your greatness becomes boundless. According to God's plan, what you are capable of achieving with your life is limitless. Your greatness must not end with you. There must always be a replica of your greatness which is not bound by times and seasons. It is called generational impact.

To have *dominion* was another command God gave to humanity. Your fulfilment is also tied to you dominating in your area of influence. Your life is a whole with several parts. Your fulfilment in ministry must not affect your family, business, or other aspects of your life. Fulfilment is taking control of every aspect of your life without any lagging. However, this will only be possible when you learn what fulfilment means and how to prioritise your life well.

To become fulfilled in life, you need to order your life according to three (3) priorities that must follow one another sequentially. A shift in the order of these priorities can affect a person's life forever. Knowing these priorities is very important for fulfilment in life. The first priority is your relationship with God. Then, your family and spouse, followed by your career and ministry.

The Lord wants you to love Him with all of your heart. He wants fellowship with you. Also, He does not want you to abandon people you call family in the process of seeking Him. You must learn to enjoy the peace and joy of togetherness in your family. Lastly, God desires that your business or ministry prospers in Him. However, if any of these is not ordered well, conflict of priority becomes inevitable.

How best can you avoid conflicting priorities? Well, the Bible showed us an example of a man who exemplified these three priorities and was successful in all. The man's name is Job, who will be the central theme of our discussion in this book. Job's family life, relationship with God and career were well managed such that each had its place and never affected the others.

Although no one desires Job's kind of life, there are many lessons to learn from him. This book will critically look into how Job was able to balance his priorities. I believe God is ready to send you great help as you open every page of this book. This book will redefine your life into a wholesome success as designed by God.

1

FIRST PRIORITY
—
YOUR RELATIONSHIP
WITH GOD

CHAPTER ONE

First Priority

—

Your Relationship With God

*'There was a man in the land of Uz,
whose name was Job; and that man was
blameless and upright, and one who
feared God and shunned evil.'*

JOB 1:1

Who are you? What do people call you? How would you define yourself? In the Bible verse above, some attributes defined Job. Everyone in Uz knew him to be a blameless and upright man. No three sentences were said about him without a link to God and godliness. Job's entire life revolved around God. His clan and the people around him could not influence him negatively. Instead, he showed them who he was through a consistent attitude of fellowship and relationship with God.

Many words could have been used to introduce Job. Yet, there was a careful selection of specific attributes to show his priority—God. Your relationship with God defines your life and gives you an identity. You are not defined by your career, profession, talent, or money. Although these things are good, they do not carry the true identity of God and who He made you to be.

Many times, we are quick to define ourselves by the things we have. God did not put His glory on things. He put it inside and on you. In you is the true nature of God. You need to understand that the Bible clearly states that a man's life does not consist of the many things he possesses (Luke 2:15). Abundant life is not found in things, but in God alone and you need to constantly be in tune with Him to enjoy this life. God was obviously in the first chapter of Job's life. It did not matter how much money Job had or how many persons served under him, the significant personality that defined Job was God.

Nothing matters in life if it is not found in God. What you are seeking is all embedded in God. Those that seek gold still feel empty after they have found the gold. People who seek fame get the fame and still feel confused about their life. But if you seek God, you may not have plenty, but you will find fulfilment for your life.

Personal fulfilment is the ultimate goal for living. You cannot enjoy life outside the directive of your Creator. Many people have subjected themselves to try and error, doing many things in search of fulfilment. Sometimes, they become successful and get all the things they desired. However, what they possess later becomes a source of frustration for them. Well, I do not mean success, wealth and other achievements aren't good stuff you need in life. I mean to say that if you relinquish your relationship with God in search of these things, you might get them, but they will never make you enjoy the main essence of life.

The true essence of life is when it is lived to the glory of your Maker. This is because God created you so that your life will give Him pleasure (Revelation 4:11). Your life becomes more pleasurable to God the more you stay with Him in the place of fellowship. Interaction with God makes you know God's mind for your life and keeps you in His perfect will. God has a will and He also has a way. God's will is His intent for your life, while His ways are His principles for your life.

> "FULFILMENT IS A SENSE OF INNER PEACE, HAPPINESS AND CONTENTMENT WITH WHAT YOU LOVE TO DO, WHETHER IT BRINGS YOU REWARD OR NOT."

Knowing God's will and ways bring you into a place of perfect peace, void of struggle and competition. But, how will you know these things if you do not have a relationship with God? Amazingly, God places in us at creation, a longing for more of Him. The more we seek Him, the clearer we see ourselves in His plans. However, the cares, pleasures and sense of competition among mankind have made many of us abandon God in hot pursue for what has already been given us in God, if only we knew.

Job did not go about looking for how he would be more successful than all the men in Uz. Rather, he stayed with God and God announced him to his world. It was evident that Job's desire for God was borne out of a sincere heart to serve God. It was not an action to impress people or show off to others. In fact, I believe Job was not living to be noticed or applauded for his relationship with God. For him, it was a usual way of life. Job would do anything to keep his relationship with God.

The Bible recorded that Job feared the Lord and shunned evil. This typifies a man whose stance about righteousness is so clear. He loved God and it was obviously seen in all his conversation. To love righteousness is one thing, but to hate sin or iniquity is another. You can love righteous acts but still have affiliations with sin. The Bible declared that Jesus loved righteousness and hated iniquity (Hebrews 1:9).

Many Christians sincerely love God but still engage in activities that are anti-God. These people love God and the pleasure of this world. They want to enjoy the satisfaction of sin and the pleasure of lust, while holding onto God. Job was not like that. He loved righteousness to its core and would always shun any form of evil around him.

The righteous Job will never join others to speak ill of God or His people. His ways were not in the path of sinners, and he never took counsel from the ungodly. Ungodliness was a natural turn-off for Job. He was a total devotee of God. He would place God first and do everything possible to keep his relationship with God.

Subsequently, men like Job in the Bible lived and portrayed the principle of prioritising God in every circumstance. They will rather die than deny God. These people would prefer to lose everything than to forget or denounce God. They denied themselves of certain things just to uphold their relationship with God, which was the core of their fulfilment in their lifetime.

Self-denial brings you to a place of personal fulfilment, where only God can satisfy you. You cannot find God when you seek other things or carry other baggage in your search. God wants you to seek Him alone and make Him a priority. Once God finds someone who relinquishes all to seek Him, He will open Himself up to such a person and bring him or her to a place of fulfilment. David was an example of such a person. Here are some of his words:

> *'As the deer pants for the water brooks,*
> *so pants my soul for You, O God. My soul*
> *thirsts for God, for the living God.*
> *When shall I come and appear before God?'*
> Psalms 42:1-2

Amazing! God was always at the centre of David's life. When your heart is fixed on God, nothing else matters to you except God. David's priority was God's presence. He

7

> **"NOTHING MATTERS IN LIFE IF IT IS NOT FOUND IN GOD."**

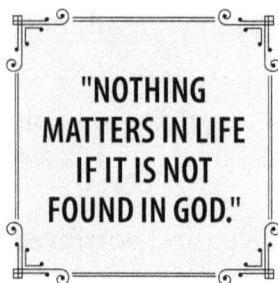

desired to always dwell in God's temple where he could worship, praise and inquire from the Lord. Little wonder he was able to rule successfully as king. You cannot make God your first and He not show forth on your behalf.

'I love those who love me, and those who seek me diligently will find me.'
P R O V E R B S 8 : 1 7

There is no partiality with God. When you make Him first, He shows up in all you do. If you relegate Him to the background, He remains there and will never interrupt the affairs of your life. The Bible says that David was a man after God's heart because he created time for God before anything else. Eventhough David was a busy king with administrative and official duties, he made God first before everything else. You have no excuse not to make God your priority.

The truth of the matter is that many activities demand your attention every time. Your work, business, and many other activities could engage your mind so much that you may have no place for God. But in the midst of it all, God wants you to make Him first.

Many Christians desire an intimate relationship with God. However, their busy schedule distracts them from making God their focus. This has become a battle in their minds. Everyone faces this battle daily, including you and I.

The Bible says:

> *'So David inquired of the Lord, saying,*
> *Shall I pursue this troop? Shall I overtake them?*
> *And He answered him, pursue, for you shall surely*
> *overtake them and without fail recover all.'*
> 1 SAMUEL 30:8

Why do you think it was easy for David to consult God first in the face of challenges? It is because he had developed the relationship and this practice over time that it had become a habit for him. Hence, your actions must become habitual first before they can become a daily life and pleasurable. What you put first becomes your priority in times of trouble. What you say in times of crisis is a function of your habitual actions. If Jesus is your priority, He will surely come first when you are in a state of confusion or dilemma.

Consequently, it takes discipline to maintain a good relationship with God. You need to schedule your time for a daily fellowship with God. Decide to be dutiful about your prayers, worship, and fellowship with God. Of course, it might not seem pleasant at the start, but consistency matters. Learn to fix a time for God and never allow any other activity to come between you and your time of fellowship. No one builds a relationship with God without discipline and consistency. Your relationship with God is a lifestyle. But until then, it must first become a daily routine and habit before it becomes a lifestyle.

What is Most Important to You?

> *"And Jesus answered and said to her,*
> *"Martha, Martha, you are worried and*
> *troubled about many things. But one thing*
> *is needed, and Mary has chosen that good part,*
> *which will not be taken away from her."*
> LUKE 10:41-42

Jesus commended Mary's ability to discern the one most important thing. It was right for Mary and her sister to have chosen hospitality over fellowship. Yet, Jesus commended Mary for choosing to sit at His feet to learn but rebuked her sister Martha for choosing hospitality. Often, most of the excuses we give for not fellowshipping with God look right and legitimate. Our excuses may make sense to everyone, but it doesn't make sense to God.

The truth of the matter is that men who served God heartily had a thousand and one reasons not to do so. Yet, they gave their all to God, despite all odds. It took a deliberate fight for them to prioritise God.

The present-day world system has a design that does not encourage a relationship with God. It is an entirely hostile environment for spiritual growth; it is infiltrated with a lot of distractions. Many activities call for the believer's attention so that the believer might forget God as the source of all things. Despite it all, you must be sensitive to know the wiles of the devil and run away from it.

There is a specific reason why our anchor text mentioned Job's dwelling place, Uz. The nation of Uz was an Arab nation in the Middle East. In fact, Job had so many businesses to take care of that the Bible called him the richest man of the East (Job 1:3). This means that there were no motivations for him to serve God in Uz. Regardless, none of these stopped Job from serving God.

The hostility of your environment towards God does not matter. The few churches around you are not an excuse. Government policy against the Church is not even an escape route. Regardless of the problem, God's expectation doesn't change. Your relationship must be kept and prioritised above all things.

> *'Now, when Daniel knew that the writing was*
> *signed, he went home. And in his upper room,*
> *with his windows open toward Jerusalem,*
> *he knelt down on his knees three times that day,*
> *and prayed and gave thanks before his God,*
> *as was his custom since early days.'*
> DANIEL 6:10

Daniel was a man who revered God above everything else. Even though his environment was extremely hostile to his faith, he kept his faith and remained dutiful to his daily prayers. A decree came to send Daniel into oblivion. It was a war against his faith. He could have backed out or relinquished his faith. However, Daniel stood with all boldness until all his enemies were silenced. The truth

is that you can never make God your first and become a
failure in life.

Whatever you prioritise will always get the best of you.
Whatever you love dearly will always get your time and
attention. In your scale of preference, where do you put
God? What is God's position in your order of priority?
What matters most to you in life? Think about this.

SEEK FIRST THE KINGDOM OF GOD

The best moments to know someone who seeks God truly
is when tough situations arise. Everyone can claim to serve
God when life is comfortable and fine. Some people turn
at the sight of tribulation. Challenges can redefine people's
faith in God. Hard times will reveal what you trust and
believe the most, if it is your God or something else.

The quality of Job's devotion to God showed at his hardest
time. He got three bad news at almost the same time (Job
1:13-20). He lost everything he had in just a day, including
his children. Can you imagine how painful it is to lose a
child? Think of how tough it must have been for Job. The
man who was once the richest in the East became a beggar
on the street.

Nothing was left for Job, save his wife. One would have
expected such a man who served God to be heavily and
heavenly defended by angels, but that was not Job's case
when the time of test came. He lost everything. You might

wonder why God allowed such an ordeal to befall a man like Job, despite his commitment to God.

God was so proud of Job that He bragged of him among His angels. The love that God had for him was so strong that He could do anything to keep him safe. Nonetheless, when the accuser challenged God over Job, and God did not retreat from that challenge.

> "YOUR RELATIONSHIP WITH GOD IS A LIFESTYLE—BUT UNTIL THEN, IT MUST FIRST BECOME A DAILY ROUTINE AND HABIT."

He supplied all spiritual strength that Job would need to stay true to the end. I believe God really sustained him from the start of the challenge until it ended.

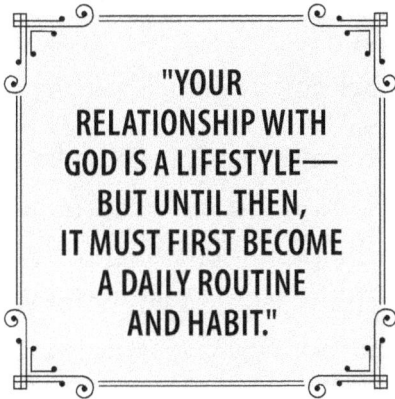

> *'Then Job arose, tore his robe, and shaved his head, and he fell to the ground and worshiped. And he said: 'Naked I came from my mother's womb, and naked shall I return there. The Lord gave, and the Lord has taken away; blessed be the name of the Lord.' In all this, Job did not sin nor charge God with wrong.'*
>
> JOB 1:20-22

Despite the entire ordeal that came upon Job in just a day, the first thing he did was worship God. Amazing! Who worships God in such a terrible situation? Job practically thanked God for losing his ten children and the loss of his multimillion-dollar business empire. He never questioned the supremacy of God. It wasn't even the time for self-pity. The tribulation for Job was another good time to worship and bless the name of God. He could have lamented first and later come back to worship. But Job gave God the first acknowledgement before anything else.

Dear reader, it is not sufficient to be a believer. Where does God stand in your time of trouble? What do you say in the face of challenges? Do you genuinely believe that all things work together for your good, or do you prefer to do it your way? Do you always find alternative means yourself when you should have talked to God about the situation? God deserves the best place and, in fact, the first place in your heart. Our God is jealous. He desires that we place Him high above all other things that matter to us.

The Bible says:

> 'But seek first the kingdom of God and
> His righteousness, and all these things
> shall be added to you.'
> MATTHEW 6:33

The many things that contend for God's place in a person's heart are God's bonuses to you as His children. It cost God nothing to add to you the good things of life, but you need to prioritise Him first. Never put your cart before your horse. God wants you to place Him first before anything else, irrespective of your situation or circumstances. Be a God-seeker.

God-seekers are desperate people who are in search of God alone. To them, there is more to know about God every day. No amount of encounter they got about God yesterday is sufficient for today. Daily, they seek to know God more and more.

> *'Speak to the children of Israel, and say*
> *to them: 'When you come into the land which*
> *I give to you, and reap its harvest, then you*
> *shall bring a sheaf of the first fruits of your*
> *harvest to the priest. He shall wave the sheaf*
> *before the Lord, to be accepted on your behalf; on*
> *the day after the Sabbath the priest shall wave it.'*
> LEVITICUS 23:10-11

The principle of making God *first* began with the Israelites. God demanded their first fruits, their first male child and the first of all their harvest. This implies that God is interested in that which seems most important to you. He is to be the first you talk to in the morning. He wants to be your first love and the first in the affairs of your home. Meanwhile, anything that God wants and desires in a person's life is always Satan's interest too. The devil is always at war with humanity so that we never make God our priority.

The devil may try to access your heart to know what you love or esteem above God. Once he finds any, he blows it out of proportion so that you magnify it more than God in your heart. The operation of the devil is just to deceive you and make you esteem material things above God.

Your love for material possession and worldly pleasure can incarcerate your mind so much that nothing else matters to you except what you desire to have. Ammon's case is a good example (2 Samuel 13). Ammon lusted after his half-sister, Tamar. This got him thinking for days so much that he fell sick. The same lust made him use a crafty means to lay with his half-sister. You see, Satan is so skilled in manipulating a person's love for natural things and uses the same to distract the individual's priority. Satan's deceits and manipulations come in diverse forms.

Paul identified some of these operations and listed them out in his letter to the Corinthian Church.

> 'For the weapons of our warfare are not
> carnal but mighty in God for pulling down
> strongholds, casting down arguments and
> every high thing that exalts itself against the
> knowledge of God, bringing every thought
> into captivity to the obedience of Christ.'
> 2 CORINTHIANS 10:4-5

A stronghold is anything addictive that keeps you away from God. They are in different shades and types. A man can be lost in imagination at the detriment of prayers and fellowship. You will just discover that the thought keeps coming and you continue to fantasise about them.

Imagination is very powerful. It is needed for every progressive work. Man must conceive ideas in the mind before executing them. However, man can also be lost in his own mind with wild imaginations against God.

The greatest of satanic operation in a person's soul is the high things that exalt themselves against God. For instance, a person could glorify religious activity above their relationship with God. You might have the head knowledge of God, but you may not know Him. The knowledge of God and knowing God are two different things. While the former is gotten by books, the latter is an experience borne out of fellowship and intimacy with God.

The Pharisees had the knowledge of God, but they never experienced the person of Christ. They gloried in how much of the law they had mastered. Jesus wasn't against the law; neither did He ever advise anyone to resist Moses's laws. In fact, Jesus was the fulfilment of the law (Matthew 5:17). But He never boasted about it. The Bible even recorded that Jesus would do great miracles and warn people not to talk about it.

Your spiritual exploit must not be placed above your relationship with God. Whatever miracle you did, always know that it was God working through you as a vessel. Your success in your personal life or ministry must first be linked to God and not your spiritual escapades.

THE KNOWLEDGE OF GOD

'Yes, if you cry out for discernment, and lift up your voice for understanding, if you seek her as silver, and search for her as for hidden treasures; Then you will understand the fear of the Lord, and find the knowledge of God.'

PROVERBS 2:3-5

Your attitude towards God is determined by the level of understanding you have about Him. The more enlightened you are about God, the more of Him you want to know. God is inexhaustible. There is no end to Him. The more you know God, the more you want to know **Him.**

> "THE QUALITY OF JOB'S DEVOTION TO GOD SHOWED AT HIS HARDEST TIME."

The man called Job was a totally devoted man to God. His desire and quest for God are seen in His daily prayers and sacrifice of burnt offerings. He practically knew what pleased and the things that displeased God. He knew how to get God's approval as he related to God daily. Job's knowledge about God differentiated him from all other men in Uz. Job did great exploits and was successful in all, so much more that his life became a threat to the devil.

God would not open Himself up to anyone who does not value Him. Jesus explained this using a parable of a pearl and a swine. He explicitly said it is wrong for you to cast your pearl before a swine (Matthew 7:7). Invariably, He was saying, do not give value to those who would not appreciate it. There is depth in God for those who are ready to dig deep. God has secrets and only those who would dig deep into God can find it.

THE FEAR OF GOD

There is an excellent difference between fearing God and being afraid of God. God is a loving father and not a dangerous deity craving to destroy. However, you must not take your relationship with Him for granted. Your intimacy with Him must not result in the sin of familiarity. God, Himself, strictly placed boundaries in the Old Testament to avoid the destruction of the Israelites. But the limitations were lifted at the death and resurrection of Jesus. Nevertheless, Jesus is not a yardstick to fear God less.

To fear God means to reverence Him as God. It is an awe of His majesty and supremacy. The Israelites' Mount Sinai experience demonstrated a full contrast between fearing God and being afraid of God (Exodus 20:19-21). The very manifestation that brought Moses near to God made the others afraid so much more that they never wanted God to speak to them directly.

God's interest is not that you become afraid of Him. He has not given us the spirit of fear but of sound mind (2 Timothy 1:7). However, He desires reverence and awe from you. What then does it mean to fear God?

'The fear of the Lord is to hate evil;
Pride and arrogance and the evil way
and the perverse mouth I hate.'
PROVERBS 8:13

The Bible described Job as a man who shunned evil. This simply means that Job feared the Lord. A good child will naturally avoid whatever displeases the parent. Job had the mind of a good child. He would do everything to maintain a good relationship with God.

You fear God when you hate whatever God hates. A person who fears God bears witness to every of God's instructions. Such an individual lives with the consciousness of God's presence. A person who fears God avoids sin and anything that opposes God. The fear of God makes you wiser and better. Let the fear of God rule your heart and no situation will ever ruin your life.

2

SECOND PRIORITY

—

YOUR FAMILY

CHAPTER TWO

Second Priority

—

Your Family

'And seven sons and three
daughters were born to him.'
JOB 1:2

Y ou cannot vividly define Job without talking about his family. After God, Job made his next priority to be his family. Job had a solid family tie. He had ten children, which were God's heritage to him. Of course, Job isn't a standard for building a home for you as a believer, but his life is a huge lesson.

Sometimes, families do not have to be people related only by blood. Your family can be anyone like a friend, neighbour, co-worker, or anybody who takes your matter to heart. Your family are people who are happy because you are part of their life as they are part of yours. They will go any length to cherish that relationship.

Your family will do anything to protect you from harm and danger. That was the case of the man Job. We can learn one or two lessons about family from him. Also, Job can be a model for raising godly children to know what to do and what not to do.

Job was prosperous as a father. He had seven sons and three daughters. In ancient times, one of the ways used to measure divine blessing was the blessing of children. Jacob had twelve, King David had twenty, and Abraham had eight children. So, Job's ten children were also an indication that he was tremendously blessed by God. That was a practice those days, which does not suit this dispensation. Even though children are God's heritage, having them in numbers does not necessarily mean God's blessing in abundance.

Today, we all claim to be sons of Abraham because of God's covenant with Abraham. The question is, are you biologically related to Abraham? No. The covenant that made you a partaker of the Abrahamic blessing is the same covenant that makes you a child of God. So, you can have children that are not yours biologically. They could be your spiritual children, disciples or mentees. In any case, anyone under your care and tutelage are your children and you must stand as a good parent for them, just the same way Job was a great father to his children.

Job was not just a father to his children; he was their priest. He would offer burnt offerings on their behalf after every feast they had (Job 1:5-6). Job always interceded on behalf of his children. He was a mediator between his children and God. As a good father, he sought the moral cleansing of his children and their reconciliation to God daily.

The Scriptures seems silent about Job's disposition to his family. Yet, it is impossible to say Job never taught his children the same conduct that made him great. Children do not only learn by hearing. They also learn by observation. In fact, they learn

> **"JOB WAS NOT JUST A FATHER TO HIS CHILDREN; HE WAS THEIR PRIEST."**

by observation more than by your words. As parents, your children will learn your lifestyle and conduct faster than the instructions you give to them. Your mentee, disciples and spiritual children learn more from your attitude and character than what you tell them to do. This is why it is amazing to see people within a denomination act like their spiritual leaders.

You are like an unconscious teacher, teaching an unconscious student. Therefore, you need to be cautious about how you live your life or else, the next generation will repeat both your mistakes and flaws as a lifestyle.

Job's consistent devotion to God would have rubbed on His children over time. Nevertheless, Job still prayed for his children as often as he could. A praying parent is a powerful one. Children are vulnerable and open to several attacks from the devil. However, it is your duty as a parent to speak to God on their behalf. Pray for grace for your children. Pray that they have the heart to love God. The best gift parents can give to their children is the gift of a relationship with God, just as Job did.

> *'And his sons would go and feast in their houses, each on his appointed day, and would send and invite their three sisters to eat and drink with them. So it was, when the days of feasting had run their course, that Job would send and sanctify them, and he would rise early in the morning and offer burnt offerings according to the number of them all. For Job said, 'It may be that my sons have sinned and cursed God in their hearts" Thus, Job did regularly.'*
> JOB 1:4-5

Praying for the children was a regular thing for Job. He did it for each of his children. Nothing is as important as setting your children apart for God. You would definitely not always be with them, but what you do for them and give them stays with them forever. If your children are a priority, you will want to show them the way of the Lord.

Hopefully, Job's home was a model to the Arabian because the Bible never recorded a day when Job and his wife had reasons for conflict in the house. Obviously, she must have been a very submissive and supporting wife to Job until disaster struck. Her reaction to Job's ailment was humane. Job's wife was just a reflection of anyone close to you who loves to see you happy all the time. Job's wife was a similitude of Peter to Jesus. Peter loved Jesus so much that he did not want Jesus to die until he rebuked that devilish thought from him because his death was the fulfillment of His purpose (Mark 8:33).

So, Job was married to His wife for many years without violence and issues. Their home was simply a godly home. Cooperation and discipline made that home. Children were raised after the same godly principle that made their parents. The parents were loving and lovable. They were role models to their children in all things.

This kind of home is still very achievable in our days. When you place God as the head of your household, He makes all things work for the good of that home. God will never lead a home into chaos. If God is in your family, joy, peace and God's goodness will forever flow in such a home.

A HOME BUILT ON GOD

A home can be built on many things. Some build their homes on beauty, logic, human intelligence, and emotional surge. All these are temporal and would soon fade away. What do you think would happen to any home that makes human reasoning their foundation? Of course, it would collapse.

Building your home outside God is like erecting a house without a foundation. Certainly, the structure will fall at the slightest wind or storm. You see, challenges of life are inevitable. However, any home built on God gets stronger and better despite difficulties. Building a house is easy, but building a home is God's doing.

'For every house is built by someone,
but He who built all things is God.'
HEBREWS 3:4

You cannot build a successful marriage without God. But then, people may say I have seen homes thrive without God. The truth of the matter is that the devil will never offer anything good. Any home thriving without God is only a time bomb, soon to explode. What you see on the face value might be happiness, but any home without God is devoid of peace, joy and God's goodness. God is the originator of marriage and you can't take out the source of a thing and still think it will thrive.

Job's successful home was 'God-made' and not man-made. He established the home on God and His word. Job's home wasn't just good. It was godly. The first underlying characteristic that makes a godly home is God. A home cannot be called godly when such is not established by God. There is a big difference between having a good home and having a godly home. While there are several psychological approaches to having a good home. It is essential to know that a good home is not necessarily godly.

A good home can be a reflection of several principles that have been tested by men. There may even be personal testimonies that support the practices of those principles. And yes, couples may live together for years and raise children who are morally sound using such principles. It all won't still make their home godly. The best it can be is a good home, but without God's goodness.

> "A GOOD HOME CAN BE A REFLECTION OF PRINCIPLES, BUT A GODLY HOME IS ESTABLISHED BY GOD."

Our standard as believers is not just to have a good home. There is a higher level to a good home, and God desires this for His children. That level is called *transcendent home*—a home that reflects God basically. The funny thing is that even godly homes come in different levels based on an individual's commitment to God. How godly a home is will be proportional to how much room such home gives to God.

Certain evidence showed that Job's home was built on God. The most obvious was his godly children. However, there are many other characteristics of a godly home that we will still examine in this chapter.

> *'Your wife shall be like a fruitful vine in the very heart of your house, your children like olive plants all around your table. Behold, thus shall the man be blessed who fears the Lord.'*
> PSALM 128:3-4

Children are God's blessings to man. They are God's battle axe against the devil. This is why the devil tries to destroy children before they get to the age of accountability.

God made Job happy by blessing him with numerous children. There must be a reason the psalmist compared godly children with the olive tree. Let us consider some features that might have suggested the comparison. The old and decayed olive tree is always surrounded by several young and thrifty shoots. This often springs from the root of the venerable parent.

These young shoots seem to uphold, protect, and embrace the old branches. They nourish and replenish the feeble parent tree. This is similar to the godly and affectionate children that gather around the table of a righteous parent. Each contributes something to the commonwealth and welfare of their old parent.

The best way to sustain anything for a long time is to pass it down adequately to the next generation. Values and disciplines of any godly parent must not end with them. It must be passed like a baton to their children. A cycle of success will only be completed when the generation after you have also been successful. God is interested in the next generation.

Subsequently, Job was successful in all things with the help of God. He knew that the way to sustain everything God gave him was by teaching his children to hear and obey

God. He must have taught them and watched them practice everything as he grew old. Job had spiritual oversight over them as their mentor and pastor. This is something every godly parent must learn.

Godly and successful parents must never keep the secrets of their successes from their children. Your children must be raised to have an interest in the things that you passionately believe. Even if they will change and choose their own interest after they have left being with you, you must still be affirmative in teaching them what you believe is right and true. Job was wise to have raised his children with this mindset. He provided all their physical and spiritual needs adequately and accurately.

Also, a home whose members hear God will be void of blight. Parenting becomes hassle-free when you teach your child to hear from the Lord. However, this kind of home does not happen overnight. Someone must initiate it in the home.

> 'And if it seems evil to you to serve the Lord,
> choose for yourselves this day whom you will serve,
> whether the gods which your fathers served that
> were on the other side of the River or the gods of
> the Amorites, in whose land you dwell. But as
> for me and my house, we will serve the Lord.'
> JOSHUA 24:15

What a noble resolution Joshua made for himself and for his household. Joshua's action is worthy of imitation in all families. He made sure his household served the Lord, even if they would be the only family. Joshua was strong in faith. He made God's Word the foundation of his home.

Job was like Joshua. Parents must model Job. There is a call of responsibility on parents and housekeepers to ensure that their subjects follow after righteousness. Hence, there is a need to train our children in the right way to go.

RAISING GIANTS—THE TRAINING OF A CHILD

Your children watching you do what you do is enough training. You must ensure as a parent that your teaching is not just passive. Training your children must be done consciously and deliberately. This will help you measure growth and their response to knowledge. Teaching requires feedback. Always learn to get feedback from your children. Never assume your children understand the message you pass to them until you get their feedback. The assumption has ended many homes in the past.

Eli assumed that being a priest was sufficient to teach his children godliness (1 Samuel 3-4). He felt his sons had learnt services to God through observation. The truth of the matter is that being a pastor, priest, and a minister does not make your children saints. You have to teach them and show them how to develop a relationship with God.

Eli was spiritually active but had no relationship with his children. He practically had no connection with his children. Eli lost connection with his sons so much more that he couldn't correct them even when their deviant behaviour were reported to him. It was very easy for God to choose Samuel over Eli's sons.

Train up a child in the way he should go,
and when he is old he will not depart from it.
PROVERBS 22:6

The discipline and infusion of godly principles into the mind are better done early in a child's life. A child's heart is like a plain sheet of paper. The child's mind is ductile, tender, and so ready for any good imprint. Parents must take advantage of this before their children become hardened. You form the young mind through seasoned and preventive education. However, the lesson most children learn come from their parents, school and spiritual leaders. Therefore, these training's outcome must be to instil obedience, modesty, diligence, sincerity, tenderness, pity, orderliness, and responsibility in their minds.

Job was a father, a teacher and a priest to his children. He would not take the chance to assume that the civilisation in Uz was good enough to teach morals and excellent godly characters. He taught his children to speak the truth always and at all costs. Job's children must have been taught devotion towards God, sobriety and chastity to themselves. Job taught his children justice and charity towards all men. The Bible recorded that Job's children would call on others to join them at their various feasts (Job 1:4-5). It wasn't just about them. Their society benefitted from the training they had.

Parents should learn to bring their children up in a way that the children are not ashamed to tell others about God. Teach them to know that service to God is not archaic. You must help them to exercise and practice your religion and virtue. Allow them to make mistakes while making decisions but learn to correct them in love. Teach your child in love until they become perfect in love. It will be hard for such a child to depart from this training when they grow old.

The best heritage any good parent can give their children is a sound education. This must also come in the form of formal education. The outcome is to help build a total child who is skilful and able to independently provide his or her need. Other personal skills like negotiation skills, refusal skills, communication skills, decision-making skills and others must be taught in every godly home. This will help children make informed decisions at every crossroad they find themselves in. Your children must be independently responsible. You must be able to predict their decision in your absence based on the education and training you have given them.

Godly children must be trained to have a good sense of judgment—their five senses are channels to their soul. Crowds of motley ideas sink into them with each idea as a teacher. They hear your views about others and their actions.

This unconsciously channels their sense of judgment. That is why they are likely to condemn whatever you condemn and value things you value.

Your definition of anything must not be biased, else, children will replicate it. Just like Job, put your religion in its highest light. Show them spiritual splendours at its peak. Tell them Bible stories and good characters of spiritual men. If possible, help them believe

> "CHILDREN LEARN MORE FROM YOUR ATTITUDE THAN YOUR INSTRUCTIONS."

and value the Word of God, then they will believe you. This will help them have judgment according to God's expectation for man.

Job taught moderation to his children. They were not feasting every day. They had boundaries even when they were so excited. Children must also be trained in moderation towards pleasure. They must know their limit and boundaries, even while enjoying freedom. Parents must always interdict loose, licentious materials, and any of such things that corrupt their values.

Raising godly children who will eventually become giants is holistic duty. It is beyond what a session of this book can cover. However, parents must depend on God for help and direction in training their children. No two children are the same, neither are their needs. God intends to raise generals from different homes and parents are instrumental in achieving this. Godly children are like olives. You will need them to strengthen you in the future.

The oldest training school and the best is the home. Sisters and brothers are the best class-fellows. Parents are the best masters. Yet, formidable obstacles, both intrinsic and extrinsic, can prevent or impede godly parental training, and you have to fight such barriers at all costs.

LOVE AND RESPECT AT HOME

> *Wives, submit to your own husbands, as is*
> *fitting in the Lord. Husbands love your wives*
> *and do not be bitter toward them. Children, obey*
> *your parents in all things, for this is well-pleasing*
> *to the Lord. Fathers, do not provoke your*
> *children, lest they become discouraged.*
> COLOSSIANS 3:18-21

True Christianity must display the effective power of refining and sanctifying earthly relationships. Doctrines of your Christian faith must reflect in your daily living. The display of love and respect among parents should influence their children to do the same. Paul admonished the Colossian family concerning what is expected of each entity, the basis of which is love and respect.

Love involves respect, and respect or submission cannot be done wholeheartedly without love. Obedience to love and respect was also preached by the same apostles to the children and servants.

Historically, the details of what led Paul to emphasise family members' domestic responsibilities in his letter to the Ephesians were not clear. However, one could conclude that Paul believed in the family's potency and it's position as a place where doctrines are strengthened. A parallel admonition was given to the Ephesian Church too.

The precepts given are elementary and obvious. Christianity is made up of every homely element. Duties are prescribed for each member of the family. The wife, the child and the servant obey the husband while the husband loves. These domestic pieties are what make any home a house of God and a gate to heaven.

Consequently, the duty of the wife is submission as unto the Lord. This means that whatever is done must be in the consciousness of rendering spiritual service unto God. Anything done otherwise is not acceptable to God.

Apostle Paul's sacred comparison of a family with the relationship Christ has with His Church is an indication that family is primarily spiritual than societal. To Paul, all human and earthly relationships should be modelled after the patterns of things in heaven. The fleeting visible life of man is a parable of things in the spiritual realm.

Submission is a reverencial act of yielding to another. It also means letting go of one's right for another. The general application of this on women is made when they lay down their names to bear their husband's name.

Jesus submitted himself selflessly and allowed humanity whom He had made to kill Him. This also was figurative. Of course, Jesus' decision was first about God's command over Him. It is so interesting to compare His submission to what is expected of every wife in the home. Submission as unto the Lord is just as Jesus submitted unto God. God must be the basis and the yardstick to measure true submission in the home. Once it is against God, then the motive must be rechecked.

The husband's duty is to love his wife unconditionally. This kind of love is not a response to her submission. It is what you show to your family, irrespective of what they do to you.

The parallel in Ephesians presupposes that a man's love for his wife should be like that of Christ for the Church. Despite how undeserving His bride was, Christ didn't withdraw his decision to be a ransom for the Church even to the point of death. Where such love exists, there won't be questions about obedience. People will offer their service without persuasion, and the natural expression of the heart will be unfeigned love. Such sacred beauty will light up the home with an aura of Christ. Bonding will be strong and each one will be independently yoked to one another. Conversations are pure in such homes and respect is real. This kind of relationship writes a lot in the heart of the children without stress.

Children are to obey their parents in all things. Love and respect should be a normal conversation every day. Job's children lived out what they saw in their parents. They modelled what happened in their home. Can your children follow after what they see in you and your spouse? Can your children pray or desire to have a spouse who replicates all that you have as their parents?

Job prioritised God and paid attention to his family. He served the Lord wholeheartedly and made his home a place of worship. His family was his congregant and his message was God.

Your Presence at Home is Significant

Several legitimate things can deny you of your time with your family. Your work or your ministry are typical examples. This is a part of your life that God designed to complement your home. They are not to create hazards or to separate you from your family. God knew you could handle it well. That is why you were not made a eunuch and sold out entirely to the work of the ministry like Paul. If you wish to have a successful home as a businessman and a priest like Job, then you must be smart enough to prioritise your home above other legitimate demands.

'Also, his possessions were seven thousand sheep, three thousand camels, five hundred yoke of oxen, five hundred female donkeys, and a very large household, so that this man was the greatest of all

*the people of the East. So it was, when the days
of feasting had run their course, that Job would
send and sanctify them, and he would rise early
in the morning and offer burnt offerings according
to the number of them all. For Job said, 'It may
be that my sons have sinned and cursed God in
their hearts." Thus Job did regularly.'*
J O B   1 : 3 - 5

An x-rayed life of Job showed that he was a man of various
engagements. Job combined farming with real estate. Those
two businesses consume more time than many other
occupations around. There is a possibility that Job was
also into trades of servants. Many of which were workers
in his businesses.

Surprisingly, Job was also a priest. It takes a priest to offer
sacrifices on behalf of others. Job must have been ranked
among the very busy men of his days. He was really busy
with his family and his businesses.

The profits from his home were as important to him as the
profits from his numerous businesses. Nothing suffered
loss. And if anything were to suffer loss, it would not be
his family. This is an attribute that you must imbibe going
forward. Your presence in the home is as significant as
whatever it is that engages you outside.

Job could have assigned capable men among his servants
to take a lead role in his family affairs. Yet, he would not
do that. He knew that the best of his servant was not

practically fit to stand in his fatherly and priestly office. No one took his place. Job's influence was so strong in his family.

Your best hands in the office should manage every other business affair, not your family. You have to be deliberate in building your home. Your absence in the home becomes an avenue for the devil to infiltrate a godly family. Satan is waiting for your slackness in the form of misplaced priorities to attack your home. You must resist him with all your might.

> "YOUR PRESENCE IN THE HOME IS AS SIGNIFICANT AS WHATEVER IT IS THAT ENGAGES YOU OUTSIDE."

Prioritising your home in this regard is a sign that you prefer every other family member to yourself. You are willing to consider the effect of your decision on them before you conclude on what to do. This will also help your children to evaluate their decision and consider its consequences on others.

> *Let nothing be done through selfish ambition*
> *or conceit, but in lowliness of mind let each*
> *esteem others better than himself.*
> PHILIPPIANS 2:3

Peradventure, you have to be unavoidably absent from home, still do not let that same thing that has taken you away engross you so much that you are disconnected from your home. Be genuinely interested in knowing everything that happens even while you are away. Do not wait until you get back to get the gist from your family.

Kindly let me share with you the story of a middle-aged man who had been married for twenty years. This man experienced a turnaround in his home after five years of marriage when he got employment in the aviation industry to work as a pilot. Before that moment, he had been having a great time with his family, but his newly found job took him away from them. For more than three years, this man rarely came home.

Then, during the Coronavirus pandemic in 2020 which necessitated a country-wide lockdown, he came home only to realise that his only son had been living on drugs. It was a pathetic story. This young man had substituted his family with his duty at work. You must never take such a decision.

Job esteemed his family better than himself and he always placed them first in all he did. If success in any business is a function of human expertise, then the success of a home will not be less. You and your family must realise that a successful home requires deliberate effort. Job had one of such homes by prioritising God and putting things in the order of their priorities. Job had a great home; You can have a much better home where God dwells. All you need is determination and discipline. The Holy Spirit is an added advantage. He teaches all things, including spiritual technology for building strong family ties. Your home has been good, but now is the time to make it godly.

> *One who rules his own house well, having*
> *his children in submission with all reverence;*
> *for if a man does not know how to rule his own*
> *house, how will he take care of the Church of God?*
> 1 TIMOTHY 3:4-5

Finally, Paul wrote the criteria for any ministerial, managerial, or supervisory role. He warned Timothy that being married is not enough. A man must be able to control his home before he can take up any ministerial position in the Church. A man that cannot manage his family is not fit to lead others. A good home manager will manage any business effectively.

So far, God must have given you specific instructions on how to take your home to the next level. However, no matter your burden to act and take the necessary steps, you must be conscious that God is the first in this matter. Building a strong godly home without an established relationship with God means you are only day-dreaming.

3

THIRD PRIORITY

—

YOUR PURPOSE

CHAPTER THREE

Third Priority

—

Your Purpose

*'Also, his possessions were seven
thousand sheep, three thousand camels,
five hundred yoke of oxen, five hundred
female donkeys, and a very large household,
so that this man was the greatest
of all the people of the East.'*

JOB 1:3

Amazing! Did you see that? Of course, I wasn't referring to the thousands of animals, assets and numerous resources Job had. Riches does not translate to fulfilment. Your riches without God leaves a vacuum in you, which only the purpose of God can fill. There are many people who have so much to their credit, yet, they feel dissatisfied with life. What do you think that insatisfaction is? How would someone have so much and yet, feel so little and unfulfilled or unsatisfied? The summary of this is that money, riches and wealth do not give satisfaction in life.

Fulfilment is only in what God has called you to do and He measure greatness through that. Therefore, before God you are great to the degree of living in your purpose and not your excelling at a skill or a business. The Bible called Job *the greatest of all the people of the East* because he had learned to stay with God and do his divine bidding. Listen to this, never try to do it your way before involving God. Let God involve you in His work and not the other way round. Whatever you try to achieve by your strength will require the same effort to sustain it, be it ministry, work or business, if God has not called you into it, you will struggle through it.

Job's first business was animal husbandry. Of course, it looks like the most obvious of all his businesses. Job's livestock was enough to describe the extent of his wealth. He had other businesses, which we will consider later.

Job understood that the business is God's and he demonstrated it through his numerous sacrifices. Whatever resources God commits into your hands multiplies by sacrificing it when it is not even enough for you. Job's business increased and he could diversify because he saw it as God's business. Do not be surprised that Job understood the peculiarity of his environment and utilised it to his advantage. It came as an inspiration for being faithful in the little God had committed to him. You do not have to run ministry by desires or work God's work by passion. God has to call you into it and that is where the increase and fulfilment comes. If it is God, you can be sure He will provide the idea, insight, and inspiration to do it well.

INCREASE IN WORK AND MINISTRY

Your work or ministry is within the environment God had placed you. Yours might not necessarily be camels or horses like Job's, it could be a skill, an innovative idea, your talent, or something unique to you that men are willing to buy. Take a lesson from Job.

> "WHATEVER YOU TRY TO ACHIEVE BY YOUR STRENGTH WILL REQUIRE THE SAME EFFORT TO SUSTAIN IT."

God gave him an insight into the needs of his environment. He knew the best means of transportation was camel and horse. Therefore, he never raised other animals like fowls and pigeons but maximised the need of his environment to his advantage.

> *'And a messenger came to Job*
> *and said, 'The oxen were plowing*
> *and the donkeys feeding beside them.'*
> JOB 1:14

Interestingly, Job did not just stop at animal breeding and transportation. He also did crop farming. Job was a top-notch business analyst who understood his environment's strengths, weaknesses, opportunities, and threats. The implication of this is your ministry could start where you are right now, but it can go global. You can start small but you must not remain small. Jesus told His disciples to start their ministry in Jerusalem first and then to the earth's uttermost part.

Job had a very large household. This description is the most bogus of all that described his wealth and businesses. Some would interpret this to mean that he had many subjects and slaves. This suggests that Job might have been engaged in the slave trade, a common trade in his days. A large household could also mean a large expanse of land. The number of large animals Job had would definitely require a vast land.

Also, Job had a factory where milk and butter were produced. His seven thousand sheep were not just eating and grazing. Certainly, Job's seven thousand sheep produced wool for clothing—a textile industry and meat for food—a meat factory. Job's animals also produced milk for butter and cheese. The milk was so plenteous that possibly, Job almost would not find a place to set his feet on in his storage room. Job himself testified to this, saying:

> *'When my steps were washed with milk*
> *and the rock poured out for me streams of oil!'*
> JOB 29:6

The same Scripture also suggests that Job was into the mining business. Surely, he was richer than everyone else in his time. The responsibilities attached to having such great wealth made Job the busiest of all men among the Chaldeans. If Job did all these businesses, then it would take nothing less than a thousand staff who worked for him and managed his businesses. This affirms that his household was huge. In fact, Job was in the spotlight and regarded as the greatest man in the East. So what comes to your mind about Job now? A rich man with booming business ventures? Of course, he was more than that.

Job excelled in all things. First, he was a successful Christian who lived among unbelievers; yet, he had no record of violence. Secondly, he was a family man blessed with ten godly children and a respectable wife. Lastly, he was the chief executive officer of a prosperous business conglomerate. All three aspects of his entire life were well managed. He placed them all in order of priority such that one never affected another.

A critical look at the entire book of Job will definitely enlighten you more on other aspects of Job's life. However, we shall limit ourselves to these three priorities that described Job for the sake of this study. His third priority was his business and his ministry.

You will agree with me from all indications that Job was a very busy man. The responsibilities on him alone were sufficient to make him unavailable for other activities. There would not have been any extra time for him to socialise. There was not even time to relax and relate with his friends. No wonder his friends were so biased and judged him wrongly when disaster befell him. It was difficult for them to ascertain what really happened that made him so miserable suddenly. This was because they had lost connection with him because of his busy schedule.

The best his friends could do was to accuse him of sin. To Job's friends, no one goes through such demotion and lose all that they have if not for sin. Praise God! Job's senses were not clouded with condemnation. He had the right interpretation of his ordeals. He knew God as the giver and the One who takes away. He had no fear for his losses, neither was there any guilt in his heart.

Busy but not Guilty

All of Job's engagements were done skilfully. Job didn't misplace any of his priorities. He lived without any form of guilt. He couldn't trace his predicament to any known sin whatsoever. He was so busy, yet he was without guilt.

> *'Even if I were innocent, God would prove me wrong. I am not guilty, but I no longer care what happens to me. What difference does it make? God destroys the innocent along with the guilty.'*
> Job 9:20-21 (cev)

Job wasn't trying to be self-righteous. He knew his busy schedule was not to the detriment of anyone. In fact, what made him busy was that he did everything the right way. Nothing clashed with another.

Job's numerous businesses were not good enough reasons to neglect his service towards God. He gave God the first place as he ought to and never exchanged any thing for family time. He was a balanced man. He was both dutiful and spiritual. Job's spiritual, family and business life should be a model for Christians. He would not miss a priestly service for a business venture and vice visa.

> *'Then one said to Him, 'Look, Your mother*
> *and your brothers are standing outside,*
> *seeking to speak with you.' But He answered*
> *and said to the one who told Him, 'Who is my*
> *mother and who are my brothers?' And He*
> *stretched out His hand toward His disciples*
> *and said, 'Here are my mother and My brothers!*
> *For whoever does the will of My Father in*
> *heaven is my brother and sister and mother.'*
> MATTHEW 12:47-50

Just like Jesus, Job would never mix ministry with family. He wasn't sentimental about his various responsibilities. He would not allow the family to distract His work. Yet, He never worked carelessly to neglect His family.

> "YOUR RICHES WITHOUT GOD LEAVES A VACUUM IN YOU, WHICH ONLY HIS PURPOSE CAN FILL."

Job's losses in a day were not because he was careless with his business (Job 1:13-22). He had capable hands to manage those businesses. Job had men who were so detailed in accounting and in giving a daily report on each of the businesses. If Job's businesses were to be audited, there wouldn't be a single fault on the entire business. An appraisal of all that happened to his business wasn't traceable to any negligence of duty.

God would never bless a man with wealth that would make that man lose connection with Him (God) or with his family. Whatever will make you so busy or take you away from God is not healthy for you. God's blessings are good and perfect. They are not to distract you or make you independent of God.

The Bible says:

> *'Every good gift and every perfect gift*
> *is from above, and comes down from the*
> *Father of lights, with whom there is no*
> *variation or shadow of turning.'*
> JAMES 1:17

God does not revoke His words. When He blesses an individual, it is with no reverse. Your business or ministry must not contend with your personal devotion to God. No busy work schedule must be placed over the joy of staying around your family. Your conscience must always judge you faithful at all times that your priorities are in the right order. Else, guilt will hurt you forever when there is a business downtime.

Do not allow History Repeat itself

'Then the Lord said to Samuel: 'Behold,
I will do something in Israel at which both ears
of everyone who hears it will tingle. In that day
I will perform against Eli all that I have spoken
concerning his house, from beginning to end.'
1 Samuel 3:11-12

Consider Samuel and Prophet Eli. Samuel was one of the channels God used to pass down His judgment on Eli, who failed as a family man. Priesthood and every other benefit attached to it left the household of Eli. God was really angry with the entire family. He practically cut them off from rendering priesthood service to Him. God raised Samuel in their place and promised him an everlasting priesthood.

Everyone had high expectations for Samuel as the succeeding prophet after Eli. He seemed to surpass all their expectations as a faithful minister. Unlike Job, who had many other responsibilities, Samuel's only work was his prophetic ministry. He shook all of Israel with his ministerial gifts. Samuel was a prophet with discernment. He was very accurate in his visions and prophecies. Even prophets respected him and probably called him the rophet of prophets. He did many things better than Eli, but he also repeated Eli's failure.

The Bible says:

'Now it came to pass when Samuel was old that he made his sons judges over Israel. The name of his firstborn was Joel, and the name of his second, Abijah; they were judges in Beersheba. But his sons did not walk in his ways; they turned aside after dishonest gain, took bribes, and perverted justice.'
1 SAMUEL 8:1-3

The Prophet Samuel became a very busy minister. Unfortunately, he was also a guilty family man like his spiritual father, Eli. Samuel's children did not follow his ways. They had their own ideas. God's intention was never to lead Israelites with kings. The best He wanted for them were judges. That was God's means of distinguishing them from every other nation around. Unfortunately, Samuel's children discouraged the whole land from being judged. Israel craved for a king because a father failed to raise his children in a godly manner. They rejected God's offer because a busy minister was guilty of misplacing his priorities.

See what a single man's mistake caused a whole nation. Samuel was busy with his work and service to God, but he was not a balanced family man. He rendered services of help to everyone else, but he could not help his household. He was heavenly laden with a guilty barge. The supposed generational priesthood office ended with Samuel because of his misplaced priorities.

As a child, I thought it was a common problem for pastors' children to be wayward. The examples around were so much that it was easy for me to reach such a conclusion. Few examples from the Bible, like Samuel and Eli fuelled my assumption. But,

> "JOB WAS BUSY, BUT HE WAS NOT GUILTY—HE BALANCED MINISTRY, WORK, AND FAMILY WITHOUT COMPROMISE."

when I morphed in knowledge, I saw several pastors' children raised to become pastors after their parents. My eyes also opened to patriarchs like Abraham, Isaac, Jacob, David, Zachariah, and others who passed strong values to their children.

A minister and a businessman are different from each other. However, they have some similarities in common. They both render services. While the former render services to men in the name of God, the latter offers services to men by his skills and expertise. Both could be so busy with their offices and forget God who appointed them, and their first ministry—the family.

In whatever God has called you to do, your family must be your first circle of influence. Your God-given values and messages must reflect in your home, then in your ministry or career. You deserve the best of God in all that He has committed to your care. God must bless you with the kind of wisdom that Job has. You should be busy without being guilty.

DILIGENCE AND DUTY

'Do you see a man who excels in his work?
He will stand before kings; He will not
stand before unknown men.'
PROVERBS 22:29

A diligent man in his business will stand before kings and mighty men. So what happens if you are already a king or a mighty man like Job? We have established earlier that Job was the greatest in his country. Surely, Job's greatness was a product of God's grace and hard work.

Job's diligence extended to his precision in what he had. The figures were clear and straightforward. He paid due diligence and attended to the number of his herd. There were times he recounted his possession. He knew what his projections were year after year. None of his servants could deceive or misinform him about his businesses. Job was a master who knew the nitty-gritty of his business. He knew what his business needed to meet up his next projection.

The Bible says:

'Be diligent to know the state of your flocks,
and attend to your herds.'
PROVERBS 27:23

Ministers of the gospel must get this lesson straight from Job. A pastor must oversee members of his fold. He is to look into their lives and condition to know what to provision to make for them. As one who has spiritual oversight, you must feed your members with the true knowledge of God's Word.

However, this can only be achieved by being studious in the Word and prayerful in all seasons yourself. You must constantly study to make yourself approved to God. You must also labour in prayers as though your entire life and ministry depends on it. God still rewards diligence. No one achieves success by being idle. Your reward will only come after hard work.

The same diligence is expected from businessmen and workers. Your business needs the blessings and prophetic declaration of your spiritual head. However, it also needs your diligence. Do not leave the total responsibility of your business on your managers. Your engagement will motivate them to work harder and be diligent. No one will run with your vision as much as you will. Your money alone won't keep the business running; your diligence will.

Apostle Paul used another concept to explain the same concept of diligence. He believed that everyone has been called into one thing or the other. There is something you have been elected to do. Due diligence is needed to make you successful at it. Paul taught the church that whosoever will not stumble must be diligent.

Therefore, brethren, be even more diligent
to make your call and election sure, for if
you do these things you will never stumble;
2 PETER 1:10

Your diligence in whatever thing you do is what makes you valued above others. Diligence defines your worth. Never expect to dine with kings when you have not developed values in your life, business, ministry, or career.

A WHOLESOME MINISTER

Being a minister of the gospel is sacred and honourable among all other professions. It is a high calling to be separated from the vast population in the world and called by God to mediate before Him and men. You should never take your call to ministry for granted.

And no man takes this honour to himself, but
he who is called by God, just as Aaron was.
HEBREWS 5:4

A minister of the gospel is like a businessman in partnership. But in his case, his partner is God. A minister partners with God to enforce His divine will and program on earth. It is not an independent assignment that can be done outside God. In fact, what makes a minister wholesome is primarily God.

The first man that had this honour was Adam. God made him and gave him the assignment to tend and look after all that He had created (Genesis 1:26-28). However, God saw that Adam would not successfully carry out his duty without a partner. So, He gave Adam a helpmeet⊠ his wife. The first earthly assistant you need to fulfil a divine assignment is your spouse. Your spouse has a lot to do with the success of your ministry. Both of you need to have the same sense of God's leading for your life, or else, your marriage and ministry might suffer.

> *'For if God did not spare the angels who sinned,*
> *but cast them down to hell and delivered them into*
> *chains of darkness, to be reserved for judgment; and*
> *did not spare the ancient world, but saved Noah,*
> *one of eight people, a preacher of righteousness,*
> *bringing in the flood on the world of the ungodly.'*
> 2 PETER 2:4-5

Noah preached the gospel of repentance for almost a hundred years. Yet, he could only convince his family to enter the ark he made by God's order. Noah's messages sounded stupid and unreal to everyone else. The technology of their days was great that they did not depend on rain for farming. So, it was so difficult to explain rain to them. No one believed him except his immediate family.

> *'Then Moses answered and said,*
> *'But suppose they will not believe me*
> *or listen to my voice; suppose they say,*
> *'The Lord has not appeared to you.'*
> EXODUS 4:1

Similarly, Moses' first fear was that no one will believe that he had had an encounter with God. The questions he asked God were more of how to describe Him to the people. Moses felt no one would believe him. Therefore, God had to prepare his brother, Aaron, who gave Moses the conviction he wanted. The role played by Aaron and Miriam, Moses' sister, cannot be underestimated in Moses' ministry.

All these were said so that you can see the importance of family in your calling. God's pattern of wholesome ministry is parallel to the family. Your home is the first place of influence—your first assembly of brethren.

> 'These all continued with one accord in prayer
> and supplication, with the women and Mary
> the mother of Jesus, and with His brothers.'
> ACT 1:14

There is none that I know in the Bible that did ministry well to the detriment of their family. It will surprise you to know that all of Jesus' family were among his disciples. One of Jesus's brothers, James, became an apostle and the writer of the book of James. All of his family members were counted among the one hundred and twenty disciples in the upper room. Your ministry starts in your home. Once that is in place, every other thing will fall in place.

Satan's interest is to attack your home the way He attacked Adam's. Satan's power becomes limited when you rise to your responsibility as the priest and minister in your home.

The devil knows that the best way to attack any of God's family is to ensure they get so busy with activities. Once that happens, he can penetrate to destroy the home.

Never get so busy to assume your home is fine without you. Check every ministration invitation with the eyes of the spirit and be sure that Satan is not behind it before you accept them.

THE ANOINTING FOR EXPLOIT

The work of the ministry is not casual. It is beyond what is learnt in school. Knowledge is fundamental and cannot be overemphasised. However, what makes true ministers is not just knowledge. There is no way you can help a man's heart through information alone.

Information only educates, but the revelation of the Spirit brings transformation. You need deep spiritual insight to bring transformation into people's lives, especially as a minister.

> 'How God anointed Jesus of Nazareth with
> the Holy Spirit and with power, who went
> about doing good and healing all who were
> oppressed by the devil, for God was with Him.'
> ACT 10:38

The first thing Jesus went for was the anointing of the Holy Ghost. It differentiated Him from every other preacher in town. Jesus was consecrated *by God* and *to God* before he started his earthly ministration. The anointing sets you apart. You need the anointing to function maximally as a minister.

The act of anointing kings and priests is a symbolic representation of the influences of the Holy Spirit. God impaled the influences of the Holy Spirit on Christ by anointing Him. Jesus Christ had the anointing of the Holy Ghost without measure, which was manifested as the power to heal the sick, raise the dead and work miracles. Jesus Christ did great things by the anointing and lives were transformed, not because He was a minister, but because He was anointed.

The anointing of the Holy Ghost and power upon a minister is the only tool for great deeds. Ministry without God's power is futile. There must be a continuous flow of power and grace to distinguish you from others. This will only happen when your heart is set to do God's work with the help of the Holy Ghost.

Patriarchs like Abraham, Moses, Joshua, David, Samuel and the host of others had a place where they met with God continuously. The secret behind their successes was their altar. The altar was a place God would reveal secrets and give them instructions for life. Also, the altar was a place of empowerment for exploits. God has not stopped empowering His called ministers for greater exploit. The secret is the place of the altar, where you and God meet alone. There are lots you can do with the anointing. God gives the anointing, but your responsibility is to remain in the secret place where you pray earnestly to be an honourable vessel for God's use in the coming revival.

YOU ARE CALLED TO SERVE

God has a lot of things in mind to achieve on earth and in men. God's method has always been to raise a man that can execute His intentions on earth. He does this by appointing men for a specific assignment. Beside the fivefold ministry of apostles, prophets, evangelists, pastors, and teachers, there are other ministries God commits to people. He also called some into the administration and help ministry, which has a broad manifestation in the present-day Church (1 Corinthians 12:28). This wide range of ministries gives everyone in a local assembly an identity of where they truly belong. Everyone has at least a place of strength and it is by being faithful and consistent in that strength that grace is supplied to do greater works.

> "GOD WOULD NEVER BLESS A MAN WITH WEALTH THAT WOULD MAKE HIM LOSE CONNECTION WITH HIM OR WITH HIS FAMILY."

'And God has appointed these in the church: first apostles, second prophets, third teachers, after that miracles, then gifts of healings, helps, administrations, varieties of tongues.'
1 CORINTHIANS 12:28

The first Martyr, Stephen, was an administrative minister, who served faithfully to share bread and support the Church. One criteria used to select him was that he was found faithful and full of the Holy Spirit. This selection gives us the standard to choose help and administrative ministers in Church.

Despite being an administrator, Stephen wasn't limited to administration. He was full of faith, power, did great wonders and preached the gospel. This shows that every ministry must lead people to Christ.

You must be able to identify your calling. Christ has a way He can magnify Himself in you. Do not strive to be known if the Lord has kept you from public ministry. God rewards faithfulness in the little you are called to do and increases your assignment at His own time. All you need is to discover your ministry and do it faithfully.

The apostles knew that they should concentrate on teaching the word and prayers (Acts 6:4). Every other thing was a distraction from their real calling. Your call is beyond that of a caregiver. You were called to preach the power of God unto salvation. You are called to turn men from darkness to light by the proclamation of Christ's Word. Your faithfulness in this will raise mature men who will meet the criteria for help and administrative ministries.

Job was a priest in his home. But you saw how God used him to preach to his friends at the latter part of the book of Job. Your service unto God must be holistic in men. You have been called to influence the world around you. You have been called to serve divinity in humanity. God has called you that you may express the glory of His name to all men. Hence, your life, conduct and teaching must reflect your call. God, who began a good work in you, can finish what he started.

KEEP UP THE GOOD WORK

An exciting fact about Job was that he stayed true to God all through his trying moment. He never allowed his situation to cause him to sin against God. He was a similitude of Christ's life in the Old Testament, who went through tribulations but emerged victoriously. Job's deeds were good and worthy of emulation. He is a pattern of patience, resilience, faithfulness, hope and charity.

Job's life radiated fruit of righteousness, even in an unpleasant situation. This defines good works. He disappointed Satan and glorified God. The devil saw a man who loved his God more than his earthly portion. This was a rare case in all of the devil's experiences with mankind.

The devil had seen multitudes who betrayed their God for money, food and momentary comfort. He had seen those who, when deprived of earthly comforts, blasphemed against their Maker. These were the basis upon which he sought an opportunity to challenge Job's priorities. Unfortunately, he failed because Job kept on with his good works.

*'In all things showing yourself to be a
pattern of good works; in doctrine showing
integrity, reverence, incorruptibility.'*
TITUS 2:7

God commissioned you in Christ for good works. Good works are works of grace that are in Christ. They are not performed by strength, neither are they created by strength. God demands that you keep up the good work. It must be reflected in all of your conversations. God's demand for His ministers is that they become a pattern of every good work to all humanity in their conduct, character and communication.

Jesus Christ lived for thirty years before he started His ministry. No wonder the writer of Acts of the Apostles spoke of Jesus thus, *'The former account I made, O Theophilus, of all that Jesus began both to do and teach…'* (Acts 1:1). God is peculiar about your teachings. Even Satan quotes the Bible. God's desire is that your life mirrors what you teach. God wants you to live out a life worthy of what you believe. God desires that your life be a fragrance of glory that attracts others to Him.

Can your life practically teach a message to your congregants? Can people read you and be blessed as though they just read an epistle? Are your children happy with your work, or they see it as a threat to their relationship with you? Job didn't make the ministry and his ventures the first thing that defined him. You need this grace to place your priorities in the right order.

4

HANDLING CONFLICTING PRIORITIES

CHAPTER FOUR

Handling Conflicting Priorities

Conflict is unavoidable in a place where differential interest is. Any organiation or group of people who will thrive must understand conflict resolution. Conflict among people must not gravitate to hatred, disinterest and quarrel. It is just to show that humans are different and have varying desires. Therefore, you must always put what you want side by side with what other people desire. Being able to weigh matters and adjust where necessary is what makes conflict resolution possible.

Similarly, there will be times that your three priorities will clash. In those times, you must learn how to lay down one for the other according to their place. It becomes necessary to understand how Job managed his three priorities effectively.

What informed Job's preference? How was he able to balance his time with God, family and business? What happens if a man chooses another pattern different from what was observed in Job's life? These are questions that must be answered in order to understand what God expects of us.

Conflict of priorities is unavoidable in the life of an individual who desires all-round success. The more the options, the more confusing it is to place one over the other. This was why David called himself a man of one desire (Psalms 24:7). Also, Paul said, *'I do not count myself to have apprehended; but one thing I do, forgetting those things which are behind and reaching forward to those things which are ahead'* (Philippians 3:13). Mary understood that just one thing is needful (Luke 10:42).

These personalities had other things and people in their lives to look after. Yet, they choose the *one thing* that mattered most to them. Their choice must have been the safest anchor for the other aspects of their lives.

There is always the *one thing* that defines the rest, even when you are surrounded by many options. This one thing becomes the pivot on which others thrive. It becomes the focal point upon which every other thing stabilises. It is the place of safety that sends regret away from the camp.

However, the Holy Spirit gives directions whenever He wants you to do otherwise. A believer led by the Holy Spirit never makes a mistake. Therefore, the first thing you need to understand is how to hear the Holy Spirit who leads you.

The Holy Spirit leads from your spirit, conscience and God's Word. You need to pay critical attention to this part of your life so that you will not have misplaced priorities. Allow the Holy Spirit to order your steps, and you will never make mistakes at all.

> **"CONFLICTING PRIORITIES ARE THE FASTEST WAY TO LOSE FULFILMENT IN LIFE."**

The Bible says:

> *'But there is a spirit in man, and the breath*
> *of the Almighty gives him understanding.*
> *Great men are not always wise, nor do*
> *the aged always understand justice.'*
> JOB 32:8-9

The leading of the Spirit was Job's most vital secret to prioritise his life. The Holy Spirit will guide you to consciously give attention to some parts of your life when you begin to drift away. There will be a time the Holy Spirit will want you to spend sufficient time with your family before going to business or ministry. Learn to flow when He leads you.

A popular minister of the gospel from Africa shared a testimony of how he received a call from his wife while he was in a ministerial conference. The wife called to inform him that she and their only son had had an accident that landed them in a hospital close to the venue of the conference.

This man of God wasn't at the conference to preach. He only went to be blessed and be prayed for by the guest minister. It was very easy for him to go check on his family and be back at the conference in a jiffy.

In all that, he stayed glued to the ministration. He was convinced by the Holy Ghost that the accident was orchestrated by the devil to make him miss an encounter God had prepared for him that day. He had a life-changing encounter with God four hours after the call. He was so blessed with healing gifts that his prayers healed his wife and child of all complications. What if he had left the conference to attend to his family?

What about the Prophet of fire, Elijah. God spoke to Elijah, the Tishbite, that Elisha would succeed him. Elijah did not waste time at his first sight of his successor. He only cast a mantle on the busy businessman, Elisha.

Elisha understood this ministerial call, but he requested for time to fellowship with his family. He went home to his household, slew a yoke of the oxen, and made a feast for his household. Then, he bid them an affectionate farewell before he arose and went after Elijah. The truth of the matter is that Elisha could have followed Elijah immediately. Still, he placed a premium on his family. However, the decision wasn't spontaneous. He spent quality time with his family before he subjected himself to the service of God in Elijah's ministry (1King 19).

Another fantastic balance of priorities was the life of our Lord and Saviour, Jesus Christ. Jesus's life and ministry had unique expressions and responses to a similar situation as that of Elisha. For Him, everything he did per time was based on the instruction of his Father. The only acceptable reaction to justify Jesus's difference in response was the fact that the Holy Ghost led Him every time. Here are two similar scenarios that pertain to His family and ministry and how he responded to them.

First scenario

'So when they saw Him, they were amazed; and His mother said to Him, "Son, why have you done this to us? Look, Your Father and I have sought You anxiously." And He said to them, "Why did you seek Me? Did you not know that I must be about My Father's business?" But they did not understand the statement which He spoke to them. Then He went down with them and came to Nazareth, and was subject to them, but His mother kept all these things in her heart.'
LUKE 2:48-51

Jesus was in the midst of a serious ministerial work here. He was expounding the Scriptures with the scribes when His parents came for him. This event was significant to create the basis upon which Jesus's ministry will thrive. It was actually his Father's business.

However, Jesus left this important ministration to follow his parents and to be their subject. The decision was spirit-led. There was a priority clash between his business and family. But, He chose his family over the business. He did this by the leading of the Holy Spirit.

Second scenario

> *'While He was still talking to the multitudes, behold, His mother and brothers stood outside, seeking to speak with Him. Then one said to Him, 'Look, Your mother and your brothers are standing outside, seeking to speak with you. 'But He answered and said to the one who told Him, 'Who is my mother and who are my brothers?' And He stretched out His hand toward His disciples and said, "Here are my mother and my brothers! For whoever does the will of My Father in heaven is my brother and sister and mother.'*
> MATTHEW 12:46-50

Jesus was also at the crux of the work here. Crowds were around listening to all He had to say. It was one of those days of doctrines establishment and cleansing by the Word. Then, His family members came to talk with him. Jesus must have left home for days. It is actually possible that Mary brought food out of concern that her son has been away for days.

But, Jesus did not only turn them down, He also preached a sermon to make them see that his first relatives are God-seekers. There was a clash between his ministry and his family, and he simply chose his ministry over his family.

These scenarios look so simple and might not have portrayed the conflicts you have experienced over time. It might not also have given you a projection of what should be expected as you prioritise God, family and work.

But, I will like to establish that you need to depend on the Holy Spirit every time to resolve your conflicting priorities. As a matter of fact, what works for someone may not work for you. You are uniquely surrounded by people who make one situation entirely

> "IT TAKES WISDOM TO KNOW WHAT TO SAY NO TO, EVEN WHEN EVERYTHING SEEMS URGENT."

different from others. Just put God first and let Him give you the direction He desires of you every time. Map out a workable plan to accommodate all your priorities.

PLANNING AND STRATEGISING

You need discipline and consistency to be yoked with God, bond with your family, and yet be excellent with ministry and business all at the same time. Each of these requires a lot of time. Unfortunately, time seems so limited to achieve all these, particularly for ministers that combine counselling and unsolicited responsibilities with theirs. The only way out is to set a plan and stick by it. Always bear it in mind that your worth is tied to your efficiency. People withdraw from you the moment you lose that flavour of excellence that makes you indispensable.

Your plan and time allocation should follow the same order we have discussed in the previous chapters of this book. God must come first in your plan. He must have the pre-eminence in your life and ministry. Even Jesus understood that people will always have needs. Therefore, before dawn, Jesus would always withdraw into a solitary place to fellowship with God.

There is every possibility that someone or something needs your attention once its morning. So, give God the early hours of your days. It will actually take extra work for you to be consistent with a daytime devotion. You can be sure that the distractions are so minimal at the early hours. Your fellowship with God enhances your spiritual perception.

Your devotion must be centred on your growth. What qualifies you as a minister is your life, not your articulation or skills. Skills naturally grow in a life that is growing. Teaching grace and powerful messages will express itself without stress when you concentrate on your growth. Allocate time for growth. Plan to read, attend conferences, study for long, and pray like your entire life revolves around it.

Your second priority is your family. You need wisdom and discernment to be faithful at home. Intimacy must be strong in your home. Yet, your immediate family must not lose that reverence that a pastor lives with them. You need time with your home as their head, just like every man is in their homes.

Do not be too busy and neglect the emotional needs of your wife. Never make her regret marrying you. Also, your children must enjoy being around you as a parent. Play with them and find time to go watch them play with their mates.

You must put their events in your calendar like it's a ministration you booked. It is easy to impact them with spiritual values when you are their friend. Plan for a vacation, visit relatives and family friends with them and have fun together. Your children must not judge God wicked for calling you into ministry.

The third to plan for is your ministry. There is much tendency to get more invitations as you grow stronger and stronger in the Lord. However, God must bless you with discernment to know which to accept and reject.

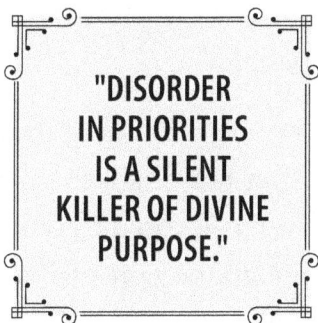

> "DISORDER IN PRIORITIES IS A SILENT KILLER OF DIVINE PURPOSE."

Satan can also orchestrate an invitation to achieve his aim. Jesus was very hungry when the devil told him to convert bread to stone (Matthew 4:1-4). Paul said all things are good, but not all are expedient. Therefore, schedule time for your personal retreat. It is wise to sharpen the axe that cuts regularly. Plan for rest too.

God is interested in His people so much more that He planned rest for them. Find time to rest after every itinerary ministration. Your body is like a horse and your word, a message. If you kill the horse, the message will be lost. Stay healthy, fit and spiritual to keep the work God has given you.

> "PEACE IN LIFE COMES WHEN YOU ALIGN YOUR DAILY ACTIONS WITH DIVINE ORDER."

THE BALANCED LIFE

You see that Job did not have many things to add to his profile. He had just three things, and none was as great as he was in Uz. He was choosy with his priorities; yet, the ones he chose made him relevant before God and his people.

Your environment may not respect your choice of priority. They may dislike the emphasis you place on God and may even call you different names. Be convinced that God did not make you to live a life designed by any man. God made you and your entire life must be for Him. People who mock you for your choices will be the same that will appreciate your consistency if you stay true.

A balanced life is a life that follows the order of life designed by God. It is a life that represents God, reproduces godly values, and reflects excellence in all. God is not interested in anything lesser than this. You have all it takes to live a balanced life.

OTHER BOOKS
BY THE AUTHOR

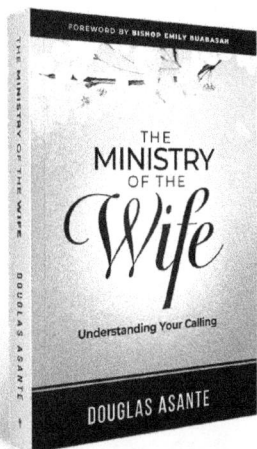

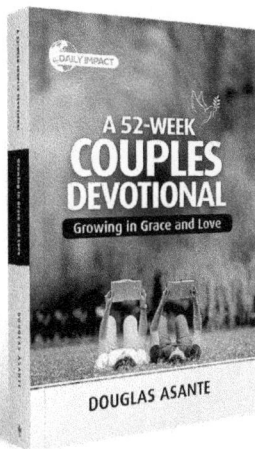

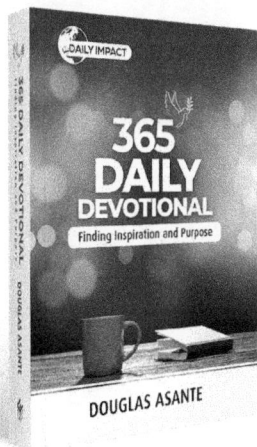

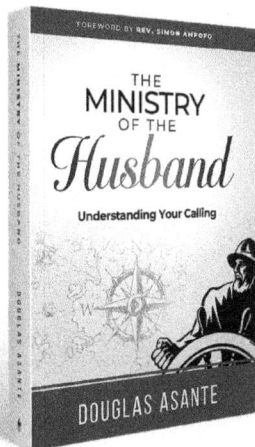

THE MINISTRY OF THE WIFE

FOREWORD BY BISHOP EMILY RUABASAH

THE
MINISTRY
OF THE
Wife

Understanding Your Calling

DOUGLAS ASANTE

---

the DAILY IMPACT

A 52-WEEK
COUPLES
DEVOTIONAL
Growing in Grace and Love

DOUGLAS ASANTE

---

the DAILY IMPACT

365
DAILY
DEVOTIONAL
Finding Inspiration and Purpose

DOUGLAS ASANTE

FOREWORD BY REV. SIMON AMPOFO

THE
MINISTRY
OF THE
Husband

Understanding Your Calling

DOUGLAS ASANTE

AVAILABLE ON

amazon   amazonkindle

www.dasante.org.uk